LIFE ON THE EDGE

A Brief History
of
Shingle Street

"Shingle Street is on the edge of the Sandlings, the ten mile border of
marine Suffolk, where we East Anglians expected Napoleon and Hitler
to arrive. So, in 1808, we took Captain Ford's advice, and built Martello
towers and, in 1938, no end of pillboxes. But no one came."
Ronald Blythe

Instead, the ceaseless enemy has been the sea.
Generations of pilots and coastguards put out in their boats to rescue
those wrecked on the shoals. Storms claimed many vessels and lives.
But the sea also provided their livelihood. Ships needed pilots, wrecks
were salvaged and fish and coal came from the sea.

John Nash

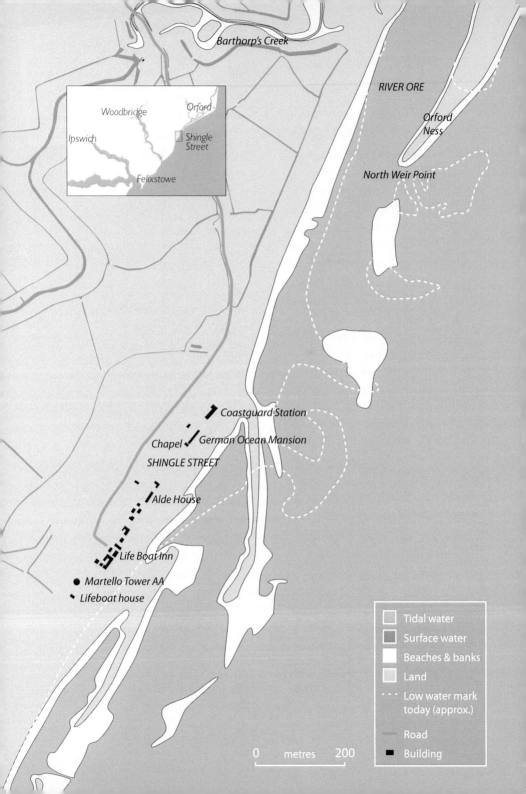

Barthorp's Creek

RIVER ORE

Orford
Ness

North Weir Point

Woodbridge   Orford

Ipswich   Shingle
                              Street

Felixstowe

Coastguard Station

Chapel   German Ocean Mansion

SHINGLE STREET

Alde House

Life Boat Inn

● Martello Tower AA

Lifeboat house

Tidal water

Surface water

Beaches & banks

Land

Low water mark
today (approx.)

Road

■ Building

0   metres   200

Location

THE HAMLET OF Shingle Street sits on a remote shingle beach at Hollesley Bay on the Suffolk coast with the Orford Ness lighthouse to the North and the Martello tower at Bawdsey Head to the South. The little settlement is perched on the edge of the ocean at the mouth of the river Ore, known for centuries as Orford Haven, and consists of a row of small houses facing the sea with a terrace of white coastguard cottages and a Martello tower. The river goes up to Orford, flowing parallel to the sea and separated from it by the shingle spit of Orford Ness. At Orford it changes its name to the Alde and continues up to Aldeburgh before turning inland to Snape. South of Shingle Street, three Martello towers cross the marsh to Bawdsey.

Above: Shingle Street in the early 20th century, seen from the south.
Opposite: Shingle Street in 1922, based on an original map for the sale of Oxley Marshes by Garrard Turner & Sons.
Map made with QGIS. Datasets © Natural England copyright. Contains Ordnance Survey data © Crown copyright and database right [2016].

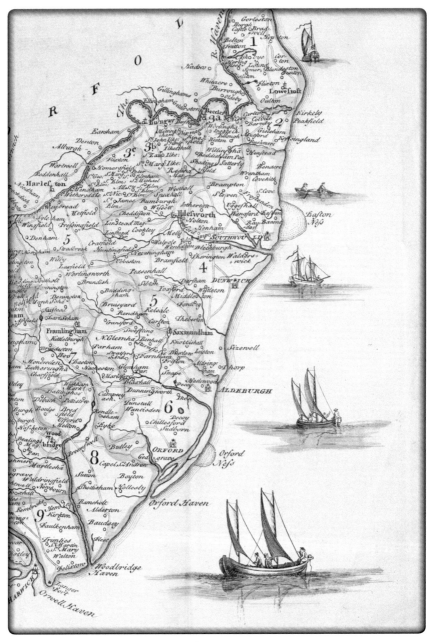

Above: "A Correct Map of Suffolk" (detail) by John Kirby, published in 1787.
Opposite page: the wreck of the 'Billy Boy Percy' at Shingle Street (photograph reference K681/1/31/ 37 reproduced by kind permission of Suffolk Record Office, Ipswich Branch).

Pilots

THE ASSISTANCE OF river pilots was essential in the days of a busy coastal trade coming into the Haven to go up to Orford, Slaughden and Snape. Many ships came to grief on the treacherous bar with its constantly changing channels or were wrecked outside it on the shingle shoals. In about 1800, a small wooden Pilot's House was built for those stationed at the mouth and this appears to have been the first construction of what was to become Shingle Street. There may have been some rough wooden huts made from wreckage used by fishermen, but a map of 1787 has no sign of buildings at the Haven.

A pilot put up a simple tavern called the Old Beach House, at the mouth of the river, as a place where the pilots and others could meet and drink. In The Reverend Richard Cobbold's *The History of Margaret Catchpole, A Suffolk Girl*, Margaret's brother Edward, while searching for her villainous smuggler lover, Will Laud, went to the Old Beach House "then kept by Jacob Merrells, a pilot", which was much frequented by the surveyors and workmen when building the Martello towers in the 1800s.

The pilots were joined by coastguards to be the core of a small community which lived by piloting the shipping, guarding the coast, saving the lives of those wrecked on the bar, as well as salvaging stricken vessels and their cargoes. They were also fishermen who lived by the sea and on the sea. It was a hard life with many risks and the storms in the bay claimed the lives of pilots and coastguards as well as mariners.

Top: the Orford Haven bar buoy today (photo: Ian Cameron).
Above: the Lifeboat Inn stood here until WWII (photo supplied by Elizabeth Maskell).

To this day, Orford Haven has a forbidding reputation for sailors. At its narrow entrance channel the tides move at an alarming rate, up to four knots on the flood and more than five knots on the ebb. In 1975 Trinity House, the ancient corporation responsible for safeguarding navigation, placed the Orford Haven Buoy with its clanging bell at the mouth of the river where strong off shore winds form a mass of breaking seas which often makes it impossible to gain the Haven. The mariners who beat their way up river headed for the calm anchorage on the landward side of Havergate Island below Orford known as Abraham's Bosom. To be safe in Abraham's Bosom had an immediate meaning which was not to do with the hereafter. The lives of those who navigated these waters were controlled and measured by the sea.

The Life Boat Inn

THE OLD BEACH House was succeeded by a larger building which was to become the centre of the community's life. The 1844 edition of *White's Directory of Suffolk* mentions "the hamlet of Shingle Street on the fine beach of Hollesley Bay where the Life Boat Inn and several houses were erected in 1810 for the accommodation of sea bathers." The settlement must have developed rapidly, though the idea that it was favoured for sea bathing came later. Cobbolds, the local brewery at the Cliff in Ipswich docks, built the pub in sections and shipped it down the Orwell and along the coast by barge to be erected close to the Martello tower. This was possible as, until the shingle bank shifted the river entrance further north, the Ore came into the sea near where the Life Boat could have its own quay for barges to moor before going into the river.

In the nineteenth century the easiest way to reach Shingle Street and transport goods from the outside world was by boat. On foot people could find their way across the marsh from Hollesley or come along the sea shore from Bawdsey, the parish in which the hamlet lay. Later a bridge was built across Barthorp's Creek and a track was made over Oxley Marshes leading from Hollesley to Shingle Street. Today you can drive down the winding lane from Duck Corner, past Dumb Boy Cottage and cross the sluice bridge to arrive on the shore facing the sky and the sea.

Defence and the Martello Towers

THE SUFFOLK COAST had known invaders ever since the Danes arrived in the Fifth Century, but it was the threat of invasion by the French at the end of the Eighteenth Century which led to the development of Shingle Street. Napoleon's ambition was to conquer England. "The Channel is but a ditch and anyone may cross it who has the courage," he boasted, and in 1798 a plan for the defence of the East Coast was drawn up. In 1801, Lord Nelson sailed into "Hoseley Bay" in 'HMS Medusa'. In 1803, 'HMS Antelope' and 'HMS Romulus' were stationed in the bay under the command of Commodore Sir Sidney Smith. Orford Haven was seen as a likely spot for invasion.

In 1805 William Pitt's Government decided to defend the coast with Martello towers, round forts named after a tower on Cape Mortello in Corsica which had impressed the Royal Navy with its ability to withstand attack. On the East Coast a chain of towers was planned from Brightlingsea in Essex to Aldeburgh. Two towers and a battery of 24 pounders were to be built to protect Orford Haven and the lonely settlement of a few wooden huts must have sprung into life with architects, surveyors and workmen. It was estimated that each tower would require 600,000 bricks, as it was

the thickness of the walls that would make them impregnable to cannon. They were nicknamed Pitt's Pork Pies on account of their shape and were hugely unpopular with the tax payers because of their cost.

In 1808, the first bricks and building materials were landed at the Haven and in 1810 the Tower Battery and Guard House were built on the site of the house now known as The Battery. The Board of Ordnance finally purchased land for the site of the towers in 1811 and, in 1812, the building of Tower AA was reported to be in progress. This is the tower remaining at Shingle Street. The war with France ended three years later and the towers were declared obsolete. Many were sold or adapted to other purposes but the Shingle Street towers were retained. By 1836 there was a signal station on Tower AA occupied by coastguards. There is no mention of Tower BB which was built on the present site of the coastguard cottages and was demolished in 1822. The estimated cost of demolition was £350 and the value of the materials recovered was £1050. The Board of Ordnance kept the freehold of the site and later built the Coastguard Rescue Station and cottages on it.

Lieutenant Chapman Wise's Chart

THE FIRST MENTION of the name Shingle Street on a chart occurs in a survey of Hollesley Bay carried out by Lieutenant Chapman Wise, RN, in 1836. This shows the Battery, Martello Tower AA and a small line of houses beside them with the name Shingle Street. He suggested to the Admiralty that a new harbour with locks should be built inside Orford Haven so that the fleet would be nearer to various foreign ports in the event of war. An advantage was that the railway was planning to extend in the direction of Orford but in the event flooding put an end to the scheme for a line. The report and the chart were submitted to the Admiralty without effect and many years later they came to light, bound with local maps, in an old bookshop in Silent Street, Ipswich.

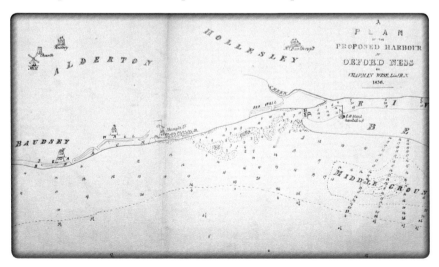

Above: the chart drawn by Lieutenant Chapman Wise, RN, in 1836.
Left: Martello Tower AA before WWII with the lifeboat house in the foreground.

The Coastguards

THE COASTGUARD SERVICE had been set up in 1822 to crack down on smuggling, with the secondary role of saving life and guarding the coast. A station was established at the Haven as smuggling was rife all along the coast. With the pilots, the coastguards made up the hierarchy of the hamlet's population. The Census Return of 1841 for Shingle Street lists three pilots and their families and one pilot's widow living in their own cottages and four resident coastguards and their families, two of which lived in the Martello tower while the others rented cottages on the beach. Coastguards did not own their houses as they were moved every few years to prevent them becoming too friendly with law breaking neighbours. The Census Returns from 1851 onwards show that the number of coastguards increased to a maximum of seven by 1911 with five Trinity House pilots. The early river pilots were self-appointed experienced sea men but later in the century pilots sought recognition from Trinity House and wore its uniform.

The lookout pole north of the Rescue Station at Shingle Street (photos supplied by Robin Baker).

A Life Boat and the Rocket Equipment

In February 1865, the local paper recorded that a small class of lifeboat had been supplied to the Orford Haven Coastguard Station "which it is hoped would prove of great service, there not being any life boat nearer to Hollesley Bay than at Aldeburgh." It was kept in the boat house beside the Martello tower but in time it proved difficult to launch from that spot. The life boat was removed and the building became a mortuary for bodies washed up on the beach.

Passengers and crew often drowned a stone's throw from the shore after a vessel had struck and early in the nineteenth century progress had been made with life-saving equipment. Rockets on the shore could fire a shot with 500 yards of line to the stranded vessel and the breeches buoy then was pulled back with those to be rescued in a sort of cradle. Many lives were saved and after the Rescue Station was built at the Haven, it housed the equipment. A lookout pole, which a coastguard could climb to see how the aim had to be adjusted if the rocket missed its target, was sited near the Station. The use of the breeches buoy by the Shingle Street Coastguards continued until the 1970s.

Smuggling

Smugglers operated all along the coast as the loneliness of the shore was ideal for landing contraband. The *Ipswich Journal* regularly reported large seizures of brandy, Geneva gin, tobacco and tea by the Preventative Officers stationed at the Haven. However, much must have been undetected because the smugglers were local men with families and connections in the villages and farms. The *History of Margaret Catchpole* already mentioned has descriptions of violent battles on the beach between coastguards and smugglers and of the fate of informers. The name 'Dumb Boy Cottage' on the road to Shingle Street has an uncertain origin. When questioned by the coastguards after a run, did the boy wisely pretend to be dumb or did he talk and afterwards was unable ever to speak again? What is certain is that the wild and violent trade went on all around the Haven.

Wrecks, Salvage and Saving Life

As THE NINETEENTH century progressed, smuggling decreased and the principal duty of the coastguards was saving wrecked vessels with their crews and passengers. The pilots continued to assist ships in distress and offer their services to bring them to safety. The *Ipswich Journal* recorded long lists of vessels stranded at Orford Haven. In 1825, four guineas were awarded to four preventative officers and four pilots for saving the brig 'Jane'. This was dangerous work. The previous year, four pilots had been drowned when their yawl capsized on the way back to the Haven.

Salvaged goods and timbers were auctioned at the Life Boat Inn or advertised for sale on Hollesley beach. In 1836, the brig 'Diana' lay wrecked at the entrance to Orford Haven and was to be sold by auction with her cargo of best timber, copper and coal. Later her anchors, fittings, sails, masts and rigging were sold. In 1855, four vessels were blown ashore by gales in Hollesley Bay, all total wrecks. A further twenty vessels went ashore and were in distress in Orford Haven. Francis William Langmaid, who kept the Life Boat Inn, organised the pilots to assist in the rescue and the inhabitants of the hamlet housed, clad and fed the victims. The *Ipswich Journal* reported that 124 men, 5 women and three children were saved and rewards were paid to the rescuers.

From the middle of the nineteenth century the coastguards' duties were to watch out for invasion and to save life from vessels in danger at the Haven. The residents of Shingle Street launched their boats whenever a vessel was seen to be in trouble. Their help was not always accepted, as in 1866 when Francis William Langmaid was ordered off the vessel 'Dickie Sam' because the captain feared a claim for its salvage. This was a fatal decision as the 'Dickie Sam' stayed at sea and sank with loss of life (Ipswich Journal, September 1866). There were other dramas. In 1880, the coastguards, assisted by the hamlet's fishermen, brought the schooner 'Jane and Catherine' to anchor in the Haven after the vessel's crew had mutinied against their drunken captain. Vessels frequently struck on the shore and were wrecked.

Floods

CENTURIES OF FIERCE storms on the Suffolk coast had washed away large towns and ports like Dunwich, which was devoured by the sea in the Middle Ages, and halved ancient boroughs like Aldeburgh whose Moot Hall, once in the centre of the town, was left on the shore. Shingle Street was not spared and its inhabitants lived with the constant threat of flooding when high tides, driven by offshore gales, forced the water across the flat shore, flooding the shingle beach and the marsh behind.

In 1880, thirty feet of beach was washed away from Shingle Street in two weeks. Extensive flooding and the encroachment of the sea cut off the hamlet from Alderton except by boat and it was feared that high tides would turn Shingle Street into an island. In 1897, a huge tide broke through the shingle to form a new river mouth.

Francis William Langmaid outside his house seated on the left with two other Trinity House pilots (photograph reference K681/1/31/33 reproduced by kind permission of Suffolk Record Office Ipswich Branch).

The Families of the Hamlet

IN THE SMALL wooden cottages beside the Life Boat Inn lived generations of related families - the Langmaids, the Nortons, the Lucocks and the Burwoods chief among them. Their descendants have supplied family records and photographs without which this short history could not have been prepared.

In the 1851 Census, Francis William Langmaid was shown as pilot and innkeeper, the start of a long association between the Langmaids and the Life Boat Inn. In his smack 'Jemima', Francis William Langmaid was involved in the salvage of many vessels until 1864 when he advertised the sale of the 24 ton 'Jemima'. He continued to rescue crews and passengers from vessels in distress in the 'Jane', named after his wife.

Another well-known pilot was Henry Lucock, who was born in 1791 and died in 1872. He owned five cottages fronting the German Ocean. The Lucocks continued to live at Shingle Street as pilots and coastguards well into the twentieth century and still retain a plot of land there.

Burwoods were recorded in the parish registers of Hollesley as far back as 1675. At some point they settled at Aldeburgh where James Burwood served on a fishing boat until 1871. Soon after that James moved his family to Shingle Street where they lived beside the inn. In 1903, their son Charles Eric married his neighbour Kate Janet Lucock, one of thirteen children. Except for his early years, Charles Eric spent his whole life at Shingle Street as a sea pilot and skipper of yachts belonging to well-off summer residents at the hamlet and he also worked as a gardener.

Bob Norton was a pilot and inn keeper at Slaughden until 1916 when he transferred to the Shingle Street Station. His young daughters, Margery and Nina, came with him in his boat and lived the rest of their long lives at Shingle Street.

In 1937, Nina Norton married Ron Harris and their first home was a

Alfred Norton, grandfather of Margery and Nina, in his uniform as a Trinity House Pilot. His descendants still live at Shingle Street. (Photo supplied by Elizabeth Maskell)

small cottage next door to the Life Boat Inn. Her sister Margery married Harold Maskell who, like Ron, became a coastguard and the two sisters lived next door to each other. Margery died in 2004 aged 91 and Nina lived to be 100 and died in 2014.

Francis William Langmaid handed over the Life Boat Inn to his son Samuel James in 1901 and lived in a cottage beside it. There is a description of him in old age in *We dare to be Poor* by his great grandson, Bill Challis:

Mother's grandfather was Francis William Langmaid, also a sailor, who lived at Shingle Street, an isolated fishing community - a lone street of windswept clapboard houses on a remote shingle spit facing the North Sea. Due to some accident he had lost a hand which had been replaced by a hook. He became adept at using this and could splice a rope, for instance, with it.....

Left: J Lucy Barwood outside Larks's Cottage (Photograph supplied by Sarah Margittai). Right: Margery and Nina Norton as girls. (Photo supplied Elizabeth Maskell).

*Top: Ron Harris outside the first home he shared with his wife Nina before WWII
(photo supplied by the Harris family).
Above: Charlie Lucock and Charlie Burwood with a catch of herring around 1925.*

Top: Robert and Daisy Norton in front of Ivy Cottage and their home, Emoh Ruo.
Above: one of the pre-WWII cottages south of the Lifeboat Inn
(photos supplied by Elizabeth Maskell).

Every Sunday, Mother with her brothers and sisters would walk from Hollesley over the marshland to Shingle Street to see their Grandparents and say, "We have come to pay our respects and may stay to tea if we are asked." Grandfather used to smile and say, 'You had better stay to tea then'..

This was the pattern of the simple life of the hamlet from its early days - one of hard work, close relationships and family ties. Some residents prospered and were able to buy property there but for many it was a life with few possessions and endless resource of making use of what was to hand: beach combing for whatever was washed up, picking up coal on the tide line, catching fish, supplementing their diet with occasional game poached from the surrounding estates, growing vegetables on the allotments and selling produce and home-made jam at their garden gates. There was little money but their descendants recalled happy family gatherings and, when hard times hit many other parts of the country and the coastal trade declined, they never went short of food.

It was at the tail end of the herring season that had been a good one for the men of Shingle Street... And what was its setting but a stretch of poppy-strewn shingle, dreary marshes, that ever-changing yet monotonous sea, men who worked on the waters and watched ashore for food and clothes for their wives and little ones, and women who rarely thought of anything but their duties as wives and mothers, and such harmless gossip as the hamlet afforded.

Watchers by the Shore
by J.E.Patterson, published 1909,
a novel set entirely at Shingle Street.

Shingle Street on Sea

By 1870, while the traditional life of the hamlet continued, there was a move to establish it as a desirable place for those who wanted to enjoy sea bathing and the quiet it offered. In April 1871, the *Ipswich Journal* advertised sites for building lodging and other houses with moderate ground rents. It was the first move to promote the hamlet as a seaside resort. In 1876 and 1877, reports were published in the same newspaper prophesying that "a very modest little hamlet, delightfully situated, with the grandest sea views possessed by any place on the Suffolk coast..." had a great future before it and in a few years could rival if not surpass Felixstowe, Aldeburgh and other places "which have assumed airs of importance". This was no small claim, as Aldeburgh was a long established borough with large houses belonging to titled families and an ancient church, while Shingle Street lacked church and school and never had been even a village. It is possible that the articles were written by Thomas Neale Fonnereau of Christchurch Mansion, Ipswich who had leased land at Shingle Street and was to build there.

In fact, preparations for the future spa were on a very modest scale. In 1876, the Marine Lodging Houses were built on a continental model and were advertised in local newspapers as having all rooms on the ground floor and arranged so that they may be made into one house or divided into four separate houses, each with a large sitting room and two bedrooms.

Other houses were built beside the wooden cottages near the Life Boat Inn and wealthy families began to come for summer holidays. Commander Hope, whose brother was Lord of the Manor of Hollesley, came to live at Alde House and died there in 1892. The Ipswich Journal reported that Judge Joseph Walton, QC, MP, was staying at his home at Shingle Street. In 1899, the Martello towers were sold to Sir Cuthbert Quilter Bart MP who had built his imposing country seat, Bawdsey Manor, south of Shingle Street at the mouth of the River Deben. The only lasting impact Sir Cuthbert had on the hamlet was to insist that the danger of invasion made it necessary for the hamlet to have the telegraph, which reached there in 1893.

In 1881, there was talk of the railway extending a branch line from Melton to a point North of the Life Boat Inn and South of the Coastguard Station, but extensive flooding put an end to the idea. Dreams of rivalling neighbouring Felixstowe faded and Shingle Street was left to continue its quiet existence as a small hamlet with some holiday homes for summer residents.

Shingle Street c. 1907, oil on canvas, 30.2 x 40.4 cm, by Sir William Nicholson.

Life at the German Ocean Mansion

In 1878, THE furniture and the South Block of the Marine Lodging Houses were sold and it became one house with the name it still bears, the German Ocean Mansion, the German Ocean being the name commonly used for the North Sea until 1914. It became the summer home of a rich Roman Catholic family, the Colleys, who arrived each summer with their large family, their chaplain, their horses and their friends. They left a detailed account of their years at Shingle Street in a book which they published privately. It was an album of memories and photographs of sailing races, tea parties for local children, birthdays, dances and religious festivals, celebrated at first in the Martello tower which was used as a chapel and then in the boat house beside the Mansion, which became a shrine.

The Colleys enjoyed life to the full and employed their neighbours in the hamlet to look after their horses, tend their garden, cook and clean, do their washing and keep a late Victorian seaside holiday home functioning at full tilt. They loved Shingle Street as the special place in their lives, "the magic spot on the East Coast of Suffolk utterly away from the world", as Lucey Colley wrote in 1913 in their book *Shingle Street by Authors and Authoresses.*

Today inhabitants can echo her words which have remained true of Shingle Street ever since her days in the German Ocean Mansion.

Scenes from Lucy Colley's book show holiday life at Shingle Street. Clockwise from top left: posing outside the German Ocean Mansion, launching yachts off the beach, a family portrait with the servants, and horses in the stables.

The Coastguard Rescue Station and Cottages

Immediately to the north of the Mansion, the Board of Ordnance had retained the site of Martello Tower BB and, in 1879, tenders were invited from builders to construct a coastguard station with a terrace of cottages for the coastguards. This consisted of the Rescue Station at the north end, six cottages and, at the south end, the Coastguard House for the Chief Officer.

Ever since, the white cottages have remained a landmark visible from far out at sea. A photograph taken around the start of the twentieth century shows the Chief Officer with his two boatmen and their wives having tea outside the Coastguard House and two house keepers in black standing in the background.

The Chief Officer and two coastguards with their wives having tea outside the Coastguard House at the start of the twentieth century (photo supplied by Sarah Margittai).

The Shingle Street Tragedy

As the Great War was about to break out in 1914, tragedy struck the coastguard community. On 1st May, seven coastguards followed the monthly custom of taking the station's cutter up river to Aldeburgh to draw their stores and collect their pay. They set off at 9am with Chief Officer HT Mauger in charge. Before returning they visited The Three Mariners at Slaughden and the Jolly Sailor at Orford and then landed at the Victorine Hut on North Weir to ring the station. They were warned that a dangerous sea was running on the bar and that it should not be crossed. However Chief Officer Mauger, who was the coxswain, decided to sail over the bar and land in front of the cottages.

As the cutter approached the breaking water on the bar, the wind suddenly dropped and the coxswain lost control in the fierce tide. They

A contemporary newspaper cutting showing four of the coastguards who drowned.

quickly dropped the sail but, before they could get the oars out and regain control, the cutter capsized in the breakers. Five men were lost in a few minutes but Boatman McCauley was able to swim and drag Boatman Goble to safety on a knoll. They were rescued by two boatmen from the station, the tragedy having taken place in full view of those at the Station and their families in the cottages.

The First World War

SHORTLY AFTER THIS tragedy, Shingle Street found itself at war and again the fear of invasion and the suspicion that anyone on the shore might be a spy filled peoples' minds. Coastal Defence Batteries were built and a small pill box with a slightly domed circular roof still stands half buried in reeds and hawthorn at Dumb Boy Sluice where the road now comes on to the marsh.

A faded photograph shows a RN lorry carrying a small anti-aircraft gun, outside the Coastguard House, guarded by a coastguard with his telescope. Perhaps they hoped to shoot down a zeppelin as these silent raiders were crossing the sea to bomb coastal towns.

A RN anti-aircraft gun beside the Coastguard Cottages during World War I.

In secrecy, great activity was going on just north of Shingle Street on Orford Ness. Runways for two airfields were constructed and the Central Flying School's Experimental Flying Section was transferred to the Ness to experiment with aerial photography, camouflage and early parachutes. In a small hut, the Constantinesco Gear was developed with calibration to allow a machine gun to shoot through the revolving propeller of the small fighting planes of the day.

There is no record whether all this was known at Shingle Street but fishermen out in their boats must have been aware of a prisoner of war camp for up to 1,000 Germans who were put to work levelling the ground for the runways.

Shingle Street men enlisted and the War Memorial in Hollesley Churchyard bears the names of Gibbs, Whyard and Langmaid.

In the eighteen or so miles from Aldeburgh to Bawdsey there is nothing except a sea plane base, conveniently placed in one of the most desolate spots in all England, and a handful of cottages called Shingle Street, a place so small that if it did not boast a pub it could not be called a village at all.

Suffolk Scene by Julian Tennyson, published 1939.

Life between the Wars

FROM 1918 TO 1939, life at Shingle Street continued its traditional pattern as best it could in the face of change. The inhabitants saw the last days of sail in the coastal trade and would see the last days of steam with the coming of the diesel engine. Pilots were still needed for trading vessels and pleasure craft but the opportunities for earning money through piloting and salvage decreased. Photographs of ships' figureheads outside the cottages were a reminder of the past. No-one went hungry but there was less money in the households. The strong sense of a close knit community held. Family photographs show women talking at their cottage doors, fishermen sorting their catch, the young sitting on the shore. The postman or his wife walked twice a day in all weathers along the sea wall from Alderton to deliver the mail, hard work in a storm, but it seems there was no question of the Post Office providing a bicycle. You walked.

One of the pre-WWII "clinker-built" cottages with a ship's figurehead in the garden on the left side of the picture.

After the Colleys left the Mansion, their chapel reverted to being an empty boat house until a Mission to Seamen opened there at some point before 1920. A letter from Frank Norton to the Diocesan Record Office in Ipswich confirmed that the chapel was well attended by the hamlet's residents and that his nephew and niece were baptised there. Services were held every third Sunday by the Reverend Vosper-Thomas, who walked from Alderton along the sea wall with the organist Cyril Sharman. The verger was Samuel Curtis, who is shown on the Census Return as a foreshore labourer.

When the hamlet was evacuated in 1940 the little wooden chapel was closed and shuttered. Time and weather and doubtless the constant search for firewood by soldiers stationed there, caused its decay and collapse. Its foundations are still just visible at the south end of the Mansion.

Evacuation

IN 1940 THE whole coast became a military zone and Shingle Street was fenced off with barbed wire as far as Deben Head. The beach was mined and once again invasion was expected. The inhabitants, mostly women and children, were given a day's notice to pack up and leave in an army lorry, to find accommodation in Hollesley and the surroundings. They were told that their houses would be locked up and that they could re-turn after the war, but the truth was very different. Soldiers broke into the houses and looted them, mainly for firewood. An experiment with fire got out of control and one soldier was killed. Barnes Wallis, of Dam Busters fame, tested a bomb which demolished the Life Boat Inn and the surrounding cottages.

Barnes Wallis (in the centre of the photo) at Shingle Street in 1943 for the bomb test that destroyed the Life Boat Inn (photo courtesy of Percy Darvell).

Among the sentries stationed on the beach was a young Welsh poet, Alun Lewis, whose poem *Dawn on the East Coast* evokes the loneliness of the deserted hamlet. He died in 1944.

Dawn on the East Coast
Alun Lewis

From Orford Ness to Shingle Street
The grey disturbance spreads uneasily
Washing the icy seas on Deben Head.

Cock pheasants scratch the frozen fields,
Gulls lift thin horny legs and step
Fastidiously among the rusted mines.

The soldier leaning on the sandbagged wall
Hears in the combers' curling rush and crash
His single self-centred monotonous wish;

And Time is a froth of such transparency,
His drowning eyes see what they wish to see,
A girl laying his table with a white cloth.

The light assails him from the flank,
Two carbons touching in his brain
Crumple the cellophane lanterns of his dream.

And then the day, grown feminine and kind,
Stoops with the gulfing motion of the tide
And pours his ashes in a tiny urn.

From Orford Ness to Shingle Street
The grey disturbance lifts its head
And one by one, reluctantly,
The living come back slowly from the dead.

Three of the war time auxiliary coastguards (from left): Eric Andrews, Ron Harris and William Lucock (photo supplied by Elizabeth Maskell).

During the war, four residents of Shingle Street were employed as auxiliary coastguards when the hamlet was off limits to the public, including the residents.

The Mystery of the Bodies on the Beach

THE QUESTION MOST frequently asked about Shingle Street is whether the Germans landed there and were met with a wall of flame or disposed of in other ways. Books by James Hayward, *Shingle Street, Flame, Chemical Warfare etc.*, *The Nazi Invasion that Never Was* and *The Bodies on the Beach* have not quenched enquiries. Speculation increased when the Ministry of Home Security File HO207/1175 was classified under an extended 75 year embargo. Under press interest, the Home Secretary declassified the file which was found to be virtually empty. Norman Scarfe, the distinguished Suffolk historian and former Shingle Street resident, commented that the only mystery was why there was a mystery.

Nevertheless the legend continues. An eye witness account, by a member of the Home Guard stationed at Aldeburgh in August 1940, states that a red alert was declared late in the month and every available man was dug in behind a wall facing the marshes. "It was a clear dark evening about 9pm when the heavens appeared to open up south of Orford Light House in the Shingle Street area. We heard a tremendous amount of gun fire and explosions. The night sky was lit up with a red glow. Sporadic gun fire went on for several hours. We received word that a German landing had taken place." *(The Secret War at Shingle Street,* by Ronald Ashford)

After the War

W HEN PEACE CAME, the War Department decided that Shingle Street was so heavily mined that it would never be habitable again but the Shingle Street people wanted to return home and Kate Burwood and others decided to make a stand. She wrote to her MP pointing out that she was a widow receiving ten shillings a week, from which she had to pay rent of six shillings a week, when she had a home of her own which the soldiers had vandalised and made uninhabitable. With delay, difficulty and bad grace the government rebuilt the destroyed homes and those who had survived were allowed to return home in 1947, although some of the new homes were not habitable.

Kate Burwood and her sister Daisy Norton (photo supplied by Elizabeth Maskell).

Eric Andrews on the beach with his boat in 1968 with the Coastguard Cottages behind.

Eric Andrews was the last resident pilot and coastguard at Shingle Street. After the war he lived with his wife Gladys (a Burwood) in the Chief Officer's house and kept his nets and lobster pots in the sheds behind the Mansion. The hand winches which can still be seen on the beach were used for hauling up the boats, as at that time the sea was close to the cottages.

In 1953, over 300 people were drowned on the East Coast when, late at night on 31st January, a deadly combination of gale force winds, low air pressure and a high spring tide resulted in a major storm surge over 10 feet above normal. Shingle Street had to be evacuated and only the coastguards remained.

In 1955 the coastguard cottages were sold. A family of six children was brought up there and other children lived in the Martello tower, in Alde House and along the Street. New life came to the hamlet as

Fish caught off the beach by residents Paul Maskell (top) and Sonny Lucock (bottom left), and by vistors (bottom right).

the members of the old order were passing away. Amongst these was Will Lucock, a veteran pilot and one of the war time auxiliary coastguards. He had married Althea Langmaid and they lived at Veronica Cottage. When he died aged 90 in 1963, the obituary notice in the local paper was headed, "Shingle Street loses a noted 'Sea Dog'".

Top: Will Lucock with his dog outside the Coastguard Station.
Above: the Coastguard Cottages and Station in the 1960s with residents using one of the winches to haul a fishing boat ashore (photo supplied by Garry Savege).

The Rescue of the 'Harle Strand'

THE SHINGLE STREET coastguards continued to rescue those in trouble on the bar and ships wrecked on the shore. On the night of 20th January 1977, the 450-ton German coaster 'Harle Strand' lost its radar in a blizzard three miles offshore, south of Orford Ness, and was swept ashore at East Lane by a Force 10 gale. At 2.00 am the vessel listed with waves breaking over the side and in terrible conditions and bitter cold the crew were winched to shore one by one by breeches buoy. All were saved. This was the last recorded rescue by breeches buoy on the East Coast and perhaps the last time it was used in England.

Wreck of the 'Harle Strand' (photograph by courtesy of Archant Suffolk).

The Coastguard Memorial

THERE WAS ONE important commemoration of the past. Mr Ramsay, a grandson of Leading Boatman Bignell who had died in the tragedy of 1914, asked where he could find a memorial to his grandfather and this led to a public appeal for funds. On 20th September 2014, a plaque was unveiled on the Coastguard Rescue Station with the names of the five coastguards who died and to record the service of all who had served there since the 1880s. Over fifty Suffolk coastguards, Mr Ramsay and his brother and a large gathering of residents were present for the unveiling, the sounding of the Last Post and to watch the Aldeburgh Life Boat cast a wreath on the waters. The station had closed the previous year and the ceremony marked the end of the long and dedicated service of coastguards at Orford Haven. A great chapter in the history of Shingle Street had come to an end.

Above: the funeral procession of the five coastguards drowned at Shingle Street in 1914.
Opposite page: the coastguard memorial plaque unveiled in September 2014.

HM COASTGUARD
SHINGLE STREET

*In gratitude for those who served
at this station 1890s to 2014 and
in memory of the Coastguards
drowned here on 1st May 1914*

*Chief Officer H·T·Mauger
Leading Boatman D·E·Bignell
Coastguards W·McCauley
W·E·Finnis and S·H·Lakin*

THY WAY IS IN THE SEA & THY PATH IN
THE GREAT WATERS
AND THY FOOTSTEPS ARE NOT KNOWN

Postscript

THOSE WHO VISIT Shingle Street, whether to fish off the beach, walk the Coastal Path, watch its rich bird life or simply enjoy its peace and the healing of sea, wind and weather, may expect to find a line of holiday cottages to let. "Do people live here?" they ask. They are surprised to find that the hamlet remains a living community, one different from the old coastguard and pilot station. The residents include writers and artists, those with a love and knowledge of nature and a passion for the sea, those who go out to work in the morning and return to relax in front of the fire in winter or to sit outside their homes in summer enjoying the beauty of the bay. The description in 1876 of "the little hamlet delightfully situated with the grandest sea views possessed by any place on the Suffolk coast" holds true.

In the past, everyday life for the men and women of the hamlet was hard and challenging. They risked their lives rescuing those in danger on the sea and depended on each other in every need. Their history encourages their successors and all who work to preserve the special character of Shingle Street and continue the unceasing battle with the sea.

27/85   'Shingle Street Martello'   Richard Bawden

Shingle Street today. Top: Windy Ridge and Kate's Cottage, clinker built cottages dating back to the 1860s or 1870s with modern additions like the tower and the glass porch. Beyond them is Alde House (photo: Jason Horncastle).
Above: the Coastguard Cottages (photo: Alec Burwood).